Mammal Finder

by Ron Russo and Pam Olhausen

a guide to mammals of the Pacific coast states,
their tracks, skulls, and other signs

Ron Russo is chief naturalist for the
East Bay Regional Park District,
Oakland, California.

how to use this book

If you've seen a mammal, go to pages 8 and 9.

If you've found:

- prints or tracks, go to page 12.

- a skull or jawbone, go to page 5.

- droppings, go to page 10 and 11.

- nests, depressions, burrows, or mounds, go to page 13.

- chew, scratch or browse marks, or other signs, go to page 15.

Dimensions   Unless otherwise indicated, dimensions given here are for length.

Key Features   On some illustrations lines point out traits which are important in identification.

Mammals in the wild are elusive. When you are hiking in the outdoors, they are likely to see, hear, or smell you first. If you do see a mammal, pages eight and nine will help identify it. You are more likely, however, to find one of the signs that indicates their presence. Often footprints (see page 12), droppings (see page 10), skulls or jaws (see pages 5–7), or burrows, nests, scratch or chew marks (see pages 13–17) will be the only things you will find to prove that mammals are around.

Mammals are different from other organisms in having fur, large brains, a highly refined sense of hearing, and a variety of skin glands. Mammals also suckle their young and spend an extended time caring for them.

Hair, body temperature, concealment

Mammals keep warm under a coat of hair or fur. To protect against winter temperatures, many mammals develop thicker, longer fur. This extra fur is shed in the spring with the onslaught of warmer weather. Deer get extra insulation from the trapped air inside their hollow hairs. Mammals can control body temperature so that it stays fairly constant by panting, sweating, and confining activity to the cooler hours. Not all mammals have the same body temperature. It generally varies quite a bit among different groups of mammals.

Mammals living in desert regions must confine their activity to the cooler nights when the chances of overheating and losing precious body water are much less. Many desert

Some mammals found in the Pacific coast states are beyond the scope of a small book and are not included here: shrews, kangaroo rats, mice, old world rats, marine mammals, domestic mammals and humans.

mammals get all the water they need from the food they eat. They control sweating, and concentrate their urine and droppings, retaining as much water as possible. Kangaroo rats have gone a step further in having developed nasal traps which remove moisture from their exhaling breath. Mammals, in any environment, that are active by night and quiet by day are called **nocturnal**. Sometimes you can spot nocturnal mammals by the shine reflected from eyes specially equipped for night vision when struck by the light of a car or campfire.

The color of mammal hair generally blends with the terrain, which helps mammals to avoid detection by prey or predators. Many mammals, like hares and rabbits, remain motionless when approached by a predator. They rely on their camouflage and motionless form until the predator gets too close. At this point, the only escape is a speedy get-away.

Quail and pheasants also use this tactic. Most mammals do not see color, but only shades of black and white. A still, well-concealed animal may never be seen by a predator, even though it may pass within a few feet. In some mammals, like squirrels, all-black (**melanistic**) individuals are occasionally seen.

Reproduction

Mammals have one of the most successful forms of reproduction in the animal kingdom. The development of the young within a placental sac provides nourishment directly from the mother and protection from bacteria. The survival rate of fetuses tends to be high as is the survival of newborns because of extended post-birth care. Although many are born naked and blind, others are ready to go. Antelope fawns are ready to stand and run within a few minutes after birth.

Antlers and horns

Some mammals have antlers or horns growing from their skulls. Male members of the deer family and both sexes of caribou produce antlers. Antlers grow externally from calcium deposited by blood-filled capillaries underneath furred skin. By late summer, growth stops and the furry skin, called **velvet**, is rubbed off against tree trunks and small saplings. (See key, page 15.) Antlers are sharpened for use and display during the fall mating season. They are shed in winter with regrowth starting in the spring.

In contrast, horns grow from an inner core of calcium-rich blood tissue. Antelope horns are shed annually, but those of bighorn sheep are permanent and grow to spectacular sizes and shapes. Males competing for females judge each others' status by the size and shape of horns, antlers, and physique. Both pronghorn antelope and bighorn sheep females have smaller horns than males.

Evergrowing teeth

Rabbits and rodents have incisors that grow continuously, an adaptation to grit in their diet which would otherwise wear their teeth to the gumline. Evergrowing teeth are kept under control normally by grit, or by gnawing action. If these animals don't have enough grit in their food, or are unable to gnaw regularly, their incisors will grow outside of their skulls and protrude from their mouths. If unchecked, these teeth will continue to grow until they turn backwards towards the skull, preventing the animal from eating. Starvation and death result.

Territories

Mammals often restrict their activities to a definite area called a **home range**. In order to get enough to eat, attract mates, and survive, mammals often defend all or a part of their home range as their **territory**. A defended territory usually has enough food, shelter, and nesting material to support a male and female of the same species. Non-breeding animals usually exist in unclaimed zones or strips found between two or more territories of their species. Territory owners usually patrol their boundaries, marking them in prescribed locations with scent, urine, or droppings. Intruders of the same species are routinely driven off. The size of territories varies from year to year as the availability of food and other essential resources changes. If food is plentiful, territories are smaller than the previous year. Territories expand in response to scarcity. The territories of non-competing species usually overlap.

Parasite hitch-hikers

Wild mammals support a wide variety of hitch-hiking parasites like fleas, ticks, blood-sucking flies, and lice. Parasites can weaken their hosts, but rarely kill them. Because some of these parasites can transmit diseases like plague and tularemia to people, it is a good idea to avoid handling dead animals, especially rodents and rabbits.

Skin glands

Mammals have five different kinds of skin glands, which serve specific purposes. Mammary glands in females produce milk to nurse young. Sweat glands help to cool mammals and get rid of waste products through the pores of the skin. Oil glands lubricate skin and hair. Scent and musk glands produce chemicals used for marking territories and communication.

Careful observation, curiosity, and this guidebook will help you enjoy the mammals of the Pacific states.

skulls

dental formulas

The dental formula for a skull or jaw is made by noting the numbers of each kind of tooth, from the front center to the rear of one side. Separate counts are made for the teeth attached to the skull and those in the jaw bone.

A formula of: $\dfrac{1\ 0\ 1\ 3}{1\ 0\ 1\ 3}$

indicates that one incisor, no canine, one premolar, and three molars should normally be present on each side of both the skull and the jawbone. This formula matches the squirrel teeth illustrated to the right.

Health and age may cause teeth to be missing. So a specimen you find may not precisely match the stated formula.

If you find a skull or jawbone, try to match it with the ones on the next page. The dental formula will appear on the page indicated.

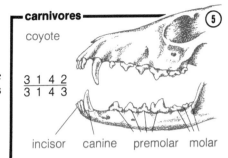

carnivores

coyote

$\dfrac{3\ 1\ 4\ 2}{3\ 1\ 4\ 3}$

incisor   canine   premolar   molar

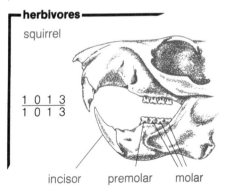

herbivores

squirrel

$\dfrac{1\ 0\ 1\ 3}{1\ 0\ 1\ 3}$

incisor   premolar   molar

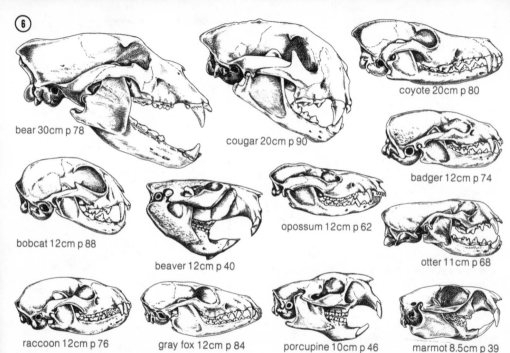

⑥

bear 30cm p 78

cougar 20cm p 90

coyote 20cm p 80

badger 12cm p 74

bobcat 12cm p 88

beaver 12cm p 40

opossum 12cm p 62

otter 11cm p 68

raccoon 12cm p 76

gray fox 12cm p 84

porcupine 10cm p 46

marmot 8.5cm p 39

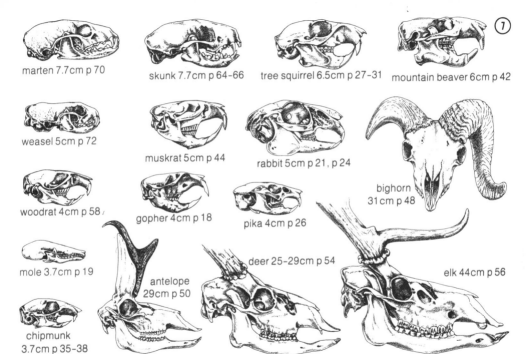

marten 7.7cm p 70

skunk 7.7cm p 64-66

tree squirrel 6.5cm p 27-31

mountain beaver 6cm p 42

weasel 5cm p 72

muskrat 5cm p 44

rabbit 5cm p 21, p 24

bighorn 31cm p 48

woodrat 4cm p 58

gopher 4cm p 18

pika 4cm p 26

mole 3.7cm p 19

antelope 29cm p 50

deer 25-29cm p 54

elk 44cm p 56

chipmunk 3.7cm p 35-38

weasel 3cm p 72

skunk 3-4cm p 64-67

opossum 3-5cm p 62

marten 5.5cm p 70

raccoon 3-5cm p 76

badger 8-11cm p 74

fox 5cm p 82-87

coyote 6-9cm p 80

bobcat 5-13cm p 88

cougar 8-23cm p 90

bear 8-11cm p 78

chipmunk 5–12 mm p 35–38

pika 3–5 mm p 26

rabbits 5–10 mm p 23–25

tree squirrel 9–14 mm p 27–31

ground squirrel 9–14 mm p 32–38

hares 1–1.3 cm p 20–23

woodrat 1–1.4 cm p 58

mt. beaver 1.5 cm p 42

marmot 3–4 cm p 39

porcupine 3–5 cm p 46

antelope 4 cm   1.8 cm p 50

1–2 cm   4–6 cm
deer p 52–55

bighorn 8 cm p 48

elk p 56   1.8–4 cm

11 cm

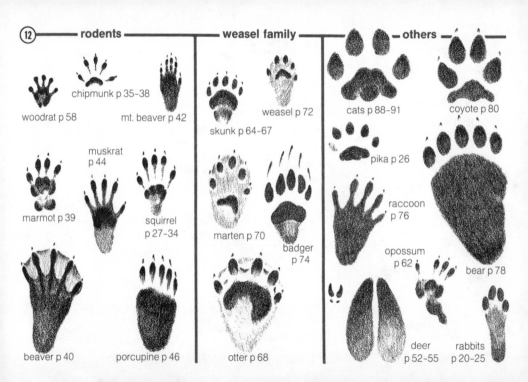

rodents

woodrat p 58

chipmunk p 35–38

mt. beaver p 42

marmot p 39

muskrat p 44

squirrel p 27–34

beaver p 40

porcupine p 46

weasel family

skunk p 64–67

weasel p 72

marten p 70

badger p 74

otter p 68

others

cats p 88–91

coyote p 80

pika p 26

raccoon p 76

bear p 78

opossum p 62

deer p 52–55

rabbits p 20–25

If you've found:

- a hole leading into a tunnel with an opening that is:

  - flat across the bottom, solitary, wider than 20cm, often with smaller round holes nearby, see badger, p 75.

  - round, wider than 20cm, with similar ones nearby, in sandy soil of deserts and San Joaquin valley, see kit fox, p. 83.

  - round, 10cm or so across, in groups of several, on hillside or flat with little or no grass nearby, see ground squirrels, p 32.

  - less than 6cm in diameter, usually at base of shrub or tree, in mountainous area, with others nearby, see chipmunks, p 35.

- a linear ridge of soil, go to this symbol [symbol] below

- round mound of pushed up soil, go to ———————————— [symbol] next page.

- a nest or house of twigs, go to [symbol] next page.

- a depressed or matted down area, go to ———————————— [symbol] next page.

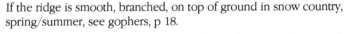

If the ridge is smooth, branched, on top of ground in snow country, spring/summer, see gophers, p 18.

If the ridge appears pushed up or caved in, in lawn or soil, see moles, p 19.

If a plugged tunnel is found under an edge of the mound, see gopher, p 18

If the mound has no obvious plugged tunnel entrance, see mole, p 19

If the nest is:

- Among high or outer branches of tree, see tree squirrels, p 27

- a cone-shaped pile of twigs, one to two meters high, at the base of trees, shrubs, in crevices, or back of caves, see woodrats, p 59

- a stack of cut grass piled under rock ledge or among rock piles of high mountain areas, see pika, p 26

- made of matted cattails or other marsh plants, one meter high, along stream or marsh edge, see muskrat, p 44

- made of stacked twigs in mounded piles two-three meters high/wide with mud packed on top, near twig dam, near or in water, see beaver, p 41.

If the depression or matted area is:

- composed of tules or streamside grasses, matted down, with tufts of twisted grass, droppings, musky odor, see river otter, p 69

- in grassland, chaparral, or next to rocks, brush, or bunchgrass, less than one-half meter long, see rabbits/hares, p. 20–25

- in meadow, forest, chaparral area, with or without strong urine scent and droppings, over one meter long, see deer/elk, p 52–57

If you've found:

- tree trunks/limbs with chew marks, gouges, or missing bark, go to this symbol below

- tree trunks with vertical scratch or claw marks, go to next page.

- tips of tree/shrub branches nipped, pruned, or stripped of leaves, go to next page.

- chewed cones, nuts or eucalyptus cones, go to next page.

- Signs that don't fit into above categories, go to ─────────── page 17.

If the chew marks or gouges are:

- Many, on one side or all around lower part of tree trunk, deep into wood, often felling tree, near pond, stream, see beaver, p 41

- large patches of bark removed, but not cut deeply into wood, often at several places on same tree, see porcupine, p 47

- linear gouges that break through the bark, but not deep into wood, extending several feet above the ground, see elk, p 57

- sharp, with shredded bark, one meter or so above ground, common on saplings, low branches, see deer, elk, p 52-57

- vertical, sharp, on underlying wood with bark torn away, two or more meters above ground, see bear p 79

If you've found:

- chewed pine or spruce cones occurring in piles in mountainous area, see chickaree, p 29

- chewed eucalyptus fruit scattered under tree, see fox squirrel, p 28

- other cones or nuts in foothills or valleys, see gray or fox squirrel, p 28, 30

If the bark has claw-puncture marks that are:

- obvious, long, usually associated with extensive damage to tree, see bear, p 79

- in sets, under 6cm wide, hard to find, see bobcat, p 89

- in sets, over 6cm wide, hard to find, see mountain lion, p 90

If you've found:

- tips of shrub branches stripped of all leaves, see deer, p 52–55

- all of the lower branches of a tree pruned evenly and horizontally, two-three meters above ground, see deer/elk, p 52–57

- tips of small shrub branches under one meter high nipped off at an angle, see rabbits/hares, p 20–25

If you've found:

- a dam of sticks across a stream forming a pond, see beaver, p 41
- piles of small pine or spruce cones next to logs or rocks, see chickaree, p 29
- a round, bowl-shaped hole in ground with wasp and paper nest parts scattered, see skunks, p 64–67
- long, muddly slides on river banks, see river otter, p 69
- partially buried droppings with scratches nearby, see mountain lion, bobcat, p 88–91
- tightly bound, twisted, cigar-shaped masses of foil, cellophane, or grass, see coyote, p 81
- any other signs, try a larger book. See p 92

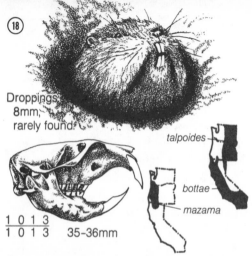

Droppings 8mm, rarely found.

talpoides

bottae

mazama

$$\frac{1\ 0\ 1\ 3}{1\ 0\ 1\ 3}$$ 35–36mm

Gopher esker: solid ridge on top of soil in snow country, no tunnel beneath.

Pocket Gophers
Thomomys bottae, T. talpoides, T. mazama

Have large, external, fur-lined cheek pouches for carrying food. Squeeze contents out with fore paws; turn pouches inside out for cleaning. Burrowing area may cover 2,000 square feet. Gophers' lips close behind upper incisors to keep dirt out of mouths while they dig. Enamel covers fronts of incisors, creating sharp, bevelled edges as backs of teeth wear faster. Gophers are active day, night, year round. Eat roots, tubers, greens. Solitary. Males fight other gophers on contact, except females in breeding season. Two species rarely live in same field. Sexually mature at three months. Young born mainly in spring, one or two litters per year, two to 11 per litter. Predation low. Enemies: badgers, weasels, snakes, owls, hawks, coyotes, foxes. Unlike other gophers, *T. mazama* spends time above ground at night and on dark days, resulting in a higher predation rate.

Mole

Scapanus townsendii, S. latimanus, S. orarius

Fur blackish-brown or gray-brown, velvety, flexible; allows forward or backward movement in tunnels with equal ease. Eyes pinhead size. Earholes concealed. Naked nose is most vital sense organ. Mole digs with broad front feet in breast-stroke motion. Can tunnel 30 cm per minute. Mounds appear to erupt from earth. Tunnel ridges collapse in time; improve soil aeration, rain penetration, reduce erosion. Mole feeds on worms, insects, centipedes, snails, slugs, some root crops. Young born March-April, two to six per litter. Active day and night. Rarely above ground, thus low predation rate.

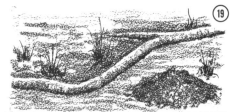

Mole tunnel: ridge of pushed-up soil or grass. May collapse.

townsendii
orarius
latimanus

$$\frac{3\ 1\ 4\ 3}{3\ 1\ 4\ 3}$$

Skull lengths:
  S. orarius 33–39mm (illus.)
  S. townsendii 41–44mm
  S. latimanus 29–37mm

Droppings rarely found.

Skull illus. p 21.

Blacktail Jackrabbit
Blacktail Hare
Lepus californicus

Gray-brown, tawny, common in sage, cactus, meadow and open grassland country. Recognized by large black-tipped ears and habit of placing hind feet ahead of front feet in normal gait. Eyeshine is red. Feeds on green vegetation, shrubs and cacti. Most active early evening and morning. Can run 30-35 mph. Uses a zig-zag running escape pattern. Young are born year round, furry, with eyes open. Enemies include: coyotes, eagles, hawks, barn owls, large snakes.

All rabbits and hares form two kinds of droppings: soft, which are reingested for vitamin and protein nutrition; and hard, which are not.

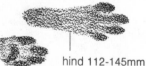

hind 112-145mm

10-12mm

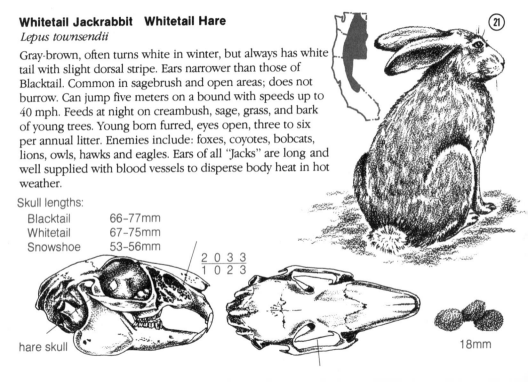

Whitetail Jackrabbit Whitetail Hare
Lepus townsendii

Gray-brown, often turns white in winter, but always has white tail with slight dorsal stripe. Ears narrower than those of Blacktail. Common in sagebrush and open areas; does not burrow. Can jump five meters on a bound with speeds up to 40 mph. Feeds at night on creambush, sage, grass, and bark of young trees. Young born furred, eyes open, three to six per annual litter. Enemies include: foxes, coyotes, bobcats, lions, owls, hawks and eagles. Ears of all "Jacks" are long and well supplied with blood vessels to disperse body heat in hot weather.

Skull lengths:

Blacktail	66–77mm
Whitetail	67–75mm
Snowshoe	53–56mm

$$\frac{2\ \ 0\ \ 3\ \ 3}{1\ \ 0\ \ 2\ \ 3}$$

hare skull

18mm

(21)

Snowshoe Hare
Lepus americanus

Changes from dark brown in summer to white in winter. Only tips of hairs turn white. Eyeshine is orange. In swamps, forests, mountain thickets. Home range about 10 acres. Nocturnal. Feeds on succulent vegetation in summer; twigs, bark, buds and sometimes frozen carcasses in winter. Does not build nest. Young born April-August, two to three litters per year, two to four per litter. Populations fluctuate dramatically, with peaks every 11 years. Life span in wild about three years.

> CAUTION: All hares and rabbits may carry tularemia or "rabbit disease" which can be transmitted to people. *Avoid handling dead rabbits,* but, if necessary, use rubber gloves.

112-150mm

Skull illus. p 21.

10-13mm

Brush Rabbit
Sylvilagus bachmani

Occupies chaparral and thick brush of coastal and foothill areas. Stays close to thickets, often clearing vegetation to bare ground along edges between brush and grass areas. Home range ¼ to one acre, with one to three rabbits per acre. Least active in middle of day, but feeds on vegetation at any time. Basks in morning sun. Young born with short, fine hair, but blind; two to six per litter, sometimes three to four litters per year, January to June. Same enemies as other rabbits; also vulnerable to dogs. Some tick species are specifically attracted to the ears of pregnant females for their blood meal, which provides the hormones the ticks need for reproduction.

23

5-10mm

Skull illus. p. 24.

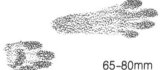

65-80mm

Mountain Cottontail
Sylvilagus nuttallii

Small, white-tailed, lives in brushy-rocky areas of juniper woodland, pinyon-juniper and sagebrush desert areas. Long hairs in uniform colored ears distinguish it from Audubon Cottontail. Nocturnal, but also active in morning. Feeds on sagebrush, grass and tree shoots. Young born naked, blind, in fur-lined nest in early summer, one to eight per litter. Rabbits in some areas produce several litters per year. Enemies same as other rabbits.

Skull lengths:

Brush	66–77mm
Mountain	67–75mm
Audubon	53–56mm

Skull illustrated is *S. auduboni*. Skulls of *S. bachmani* and *S. nuttallii* have different lattice work here:

7–9mm

Hindfoot: 88–100mm, illus. p 23.

$$\frac{2\quad0\quad3\quad3}{1\quad0\quad2\quad3}$$

Audubon Cottontail
Desert Cottontail
Sylvilagus audubonii

Dark ear tips, larger size, and white-tipped hairs on underside distinguish it from Brush Rabbits. In open plains, foothills, low valleys, coastal areas; in grass, sage, pinyon-juniper, moist chaparral. Home range one acre for females, up to 15 acres for males. Active in late afternoon, night and early morning. Stays close to thickets. Eats green vegetation and a variety of fruit, but rarely tree bark. Young born naked and blind, in fur nests, throughout the year. May live two years in wild. Vulnerable to marauding domestic dogs.

8mm.

Skull illus. p 24.

75-100mm

hind 25-35mm

25mm   3-5mm

Pika, Cony, Rock Rabbit, Piping Hare
Ochotona princeps

Round body, short legs and ears, and dense fur conserve body heat. No visible tail. Common on alpine and fir forest talus slides. Variable color blends with rocks. Territorial. Presence indicated by its sharp, nasal chirps, and by "hay piles" of drying vegetation (each one may be a bushel or more). Diurnal. Does not hibernate. Active under snow, using stored hay for food. Reingests soft droppings for protein, energy, and vitamins. Stores dried marmot droppings for same use. Concentrates urine to conserve water; leaves distinctive white marks on rocks. Young born May-August, naked, blind, three to four per annual litter. Enemies: weasels, martens, coyotes, hawks.

40-45mm

$$\frac{2\ 0\ 2\ 3}{1\ 0\ 2\ 3} \text{ or } \frac{2\ 0\ 3\ 2}{1\ 0\ 2\ 3}$$

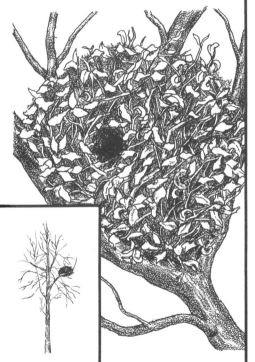

Squirrels

There are about 11 species of ground and tree squirrels. Most do not hibernate, but sleep for short periods. Eat variety of green vegetation, seeds, nuts, fruit, flowers, bulbs, roots, fungi, bird eggs, insects, baby birds, and occasionally fresh road kills. Most store food for use after awakening from sleep periods and in spring. Enemies include coyotes, foxes, bobcats, martens, fishers, weasels, hawks, owls and large snakes.

Several species gnaw cones for nuts and sweet sap.

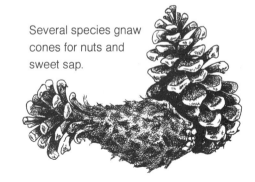

10-12mm

Fox Squirrel
Sciurus niger

Rusty, reddish gray, lower parts rusty yellow or orange; some pure gray, no rust. Melanistic forms occur. Introduced from east to city parks and campuses, now widespread in urban areas. Replaces native western gray squirrel as range extends. Like western gray squirrel, buries acorns and pine nuts, some of which are not retrieved and grow into trees. Young born February-March, sometimes June-July, two to four per litter, with two litters per year. Lifespan about seven years.

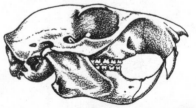

62-70mm $\frac{1\ 0\ 1\ 3}{1\ 0\ 1\ 3}$ or $\frac{1\ 0\ 2\ 3}{1\ 0\ 1\ 3}$ hind 50mm

Chickaree
Douglas Squirrel
Tamiasciurus douglasi

Dark olive-gray, grayer in winter, hairs sometimes red-tipped. Light yellowish or rusty belly. Black line along side is distinct in summer, less so in winter. In conifer forests in pine, spruce, fir, hemlock zones. Active all day. Very noisy. Feeds heavily on truffles and turpentine-flavored nuts of conifer cones. Stockpiles large numbers of pine cones near rocks and logs in fall for winter and spring use. One cache of 1,242 sequoia cones has been found. Young are born June and October, four to eight per litter, one or two litters per year.

hind 50-55mm

6-10mm

47-50mm

$$\frac{1\ 0\ 1\ 3}{1\ 0\ 1\ 3} \text{ or } \frac{1\ 0\ 2\ 3}{1\ 0\ 1\ 3}$$

(29)

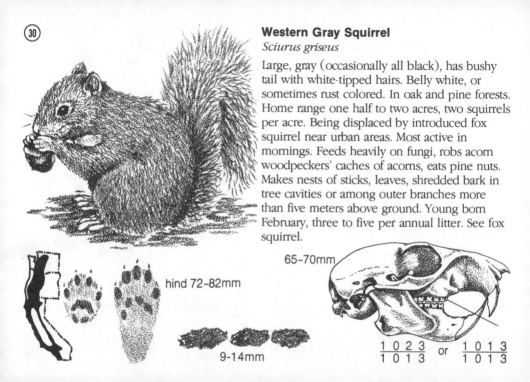

Western Gray Squirrel
Sciurus griseus

Large, gray (occasionally all black), has bushy tail with white-tipped hairs. Belly white, or sometimes rust colored. In oak and pine forests. Home range one half to two acres, two squirrels per acre. Being displaced by introduced fox squirrel near urban areas. Most active in mornings. Feeds heavily on fungi, robs acorn woodpeckers' caches of acorns, eats pine nuts. Makes nests of sticks, leaves, shredded bark in tree cavities or among outer branches more than five meters above ground. Young born February, three to five per annual litter. See fox squirrel.

hind 72–82mm

9–14mm

65–70mm

$\frac{1\ 0\ 2\ 3}{1\ 0\ 1\ 3}$ or $\frac{1\ 0\ 1\ 3}{1\ 0\ 1\ 3}$

Northern Flying Squirrel
Glaucomys sabrinus

Body gray-brown, belly hairs white-tipped, with fur-covered skin membrane between fore and hind limbs used for gliding. In coniferous and mixed forests. Home range about four acres. The only nocturnal squirrel. Eats lots of fungi in summer, lichens in winter. Gregarious in winter, may den in groups. Nests in old woodpecker holes or other tree cavities. Young born May-June, two to six per annual litter. Worst enemy: owls.

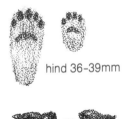

hind 36-39mm

4-12mm

40-42mm

$$\frac{1 \quad 0 \quad 2 \quad 3}{1 \quad 0 \quad 1 \quad 3}$$

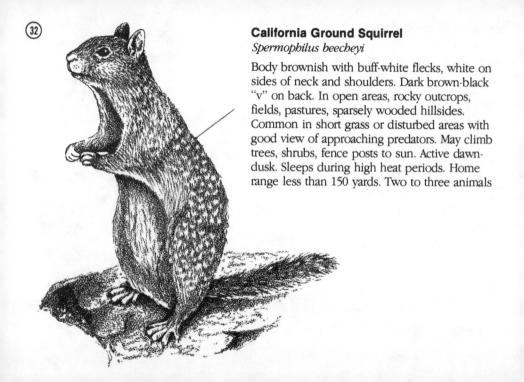

California Ground Squirrel
Spermophilus beecheyi

Body brownish with buff-white flecks, white on sides of neck and shoulders. Dark brown-black "v" on back. In open areas, rocky outcrops, fields, pastures, sparsely wooded hillsides. Common in short grass or disturbed areas with good view of approaching predators. May climb trees, shrubs, fence posts to sun. Active dawn-dusk. Sleeps during high heat periods. Home range less than 150 yards. Two to three animals

51-62mm

$$\frac{1\ 0\ 2\ 3}{1\ 0\ 1\ 3}$$

per acre; many more in some areas. Hibernates November-February in snow country. Eats variety of vegetable matter, occasionally quail eggs, chicks and fresh roadkills. Young born four to 15 per litter, spring-fall. Badgers and rattlesnakes are major enemies. In some parts of California, half of all young produced in a season are eaten by rattlesnakes. Ground squirrel's fleas can carry bubonic plague.

10-14mm

hind 50-64mm

Golden-mantled Ground Squirrel
Spermophilus lateralis

Chipmunk-like. Back gray-brown, belly white, head and shoulders golden yellow, sides white with two black borders. In moist conifer forests to above timberline. Home range less than 200 yards with two to five animals per acre. Burrows to 30 meters long, branched, with round openings near logs, stumps, tree roots or boulders. Young born early summer, two to eight per annual litter. Prepares for hibernation by adding layer of fat in fall. Cleans self by rolling in dust, then combing fur with teeth and claws.

golden yellow to yellow orange

41–44mm

$\frac{1\ 0\ 2\ 3}{1\ 0\ 1\ 3}$

12–14mm

hind 37–44mm

Chipmunks

About eleven species in the Pacific States. Some are distinguishable only by bone characteristics, geography, habitat. All have internal cheek pouches for food gathering. All are diurnal. Instead of storing body fat like true hibernators, chipmunks store large quantities of food in burrows for use during waking periods and in early spring. Inactive for short periods. Gestation takes about one month. Young born in spring, two to seven per litter, usually one litter per year. Life span about five years. Enemies: hawks, weasels, bobcats, coyotes and snakes.

$$\frac{1\ 0\ 2\ 3}{1\ 0\ 1\ 3}$$

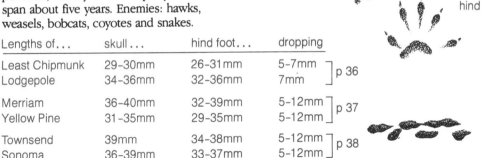

front

hind

Lengths of...	skull...	hind foot...	dropping	
Least Chipmunk	29–30mm	26–31mm	5–7mm	⎫ p 36
Lodgepole	34–36mm	32–36mm	7mm	⎭
Merriam	36–40mm	32–39mm	5–12mm	⎫ p 37
Yellow Pine	31–35mm	29–35mm	5–12mm	⎭
Townsend	39mm	34–38mm	5–12mm	⎫ p 38
Sonoma	36–39mm	33–37mm	5–12mm	⎭

Least Chipmunk
Eutamias minimus
Color varies from yellowish-gray with tawny dark stripes to rich gray-tawny with black stripes. Sides often orange-brown. Lightest colored of all chipmunks. In low sagebrush deserts to high mountain conifer forests. Nests beneath stumps, logs, rocks, in ground. Lines burrow and nest with moss, lichens, grass and feathers. Runs with tail up.

Lodgepole Chipmunk
Eutamias speciosus
Brightly colored with light-dark contrasting colors, side stripes white and dark brown. In lodgepole pine forests, adjacent chaparral, red fir forests. Eats manzanita flowers, berries, nuts, fungi and caterpillars.

Merriam Chipmunk
Eutamias merriami

Large, grayish-brown, with indistinct stripes.
On chaparral slopes, in mixed oak
woodlands, bull pines, stream thickets,
outcrops in foothills. Food similar to that of
other chipmunks. Two color forms exist in
range: those in humid areas tend to be
darker than those in arid areas.

Yellow Pine Chipmunk
Eutamias amoenus

Colors bright tawny to pink-cinnamon,
black and white back and side stripes; ears
black in front, white in back. In open
conifer forests, chaparral, rocky areas with
brush or pines. One cache of food
contained 67,970 items with 15 different
kinds of seeds, corn, and a piece of
bumblebee.

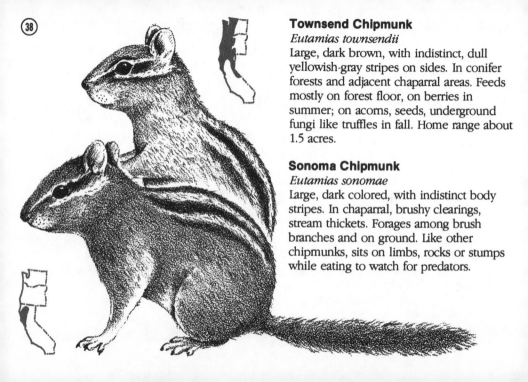

Townsend Chipmunk
Eutamias townsendii
Large, dark brown, with indistinct, dull yellowish-gray stripes on sides. In conifer forests and adjacent chaparral areas. Feeds mostly on forest floor, on berries in summer; on acorns, seeds, underground fungi like truffles in fall. Home range about 1.5 acres.

Sonoma Chipmunk
Eutamias sonomae
Large, dark colored, with indistinct body stripes. In chaparral, brushy clearings, stream thickets. Forages among brush branches and on ground. Like other chipmunks, sits on limbs, rocks or stumps while eating to watch for predators.

Yellow-bellied Marmot
Marmota flaviventris

Heavy-bodied rodent common on talus slopes and roadside rock piles in high mountains. Shares habitat with pikas. Body yellow-brown. All-black individuals occur. Burrow entrance to 23 cm wide, with fan of packed dirt. Marmot dens in talus pile. Nearby large boulder is used as lookout. Marmot chirps or whistles when alarmed. Often in colonies with a dominant male who may have harem of several females. Eats green vegetation. Diurnal. Develops layer of fat for hibernation October-March. One litter of three-six blind, naked young born in April. Lifespan to about 10 years. Enemies: eagles, coyotes, bobcats, lions.

$\frac{1\ 0\ 2\ 3}{1\ 0\ 1\ 3}$

80-91mm

28-40mm

hind 70-90 mm

Beaver
Castor canadensis

Large, dark brown rodent with scaly tail. Skull with chestnut brown incisors. Lives in mountain streams, ponds, lakes. Its transparent eyelids cover eyes during dives to allow continuous vision while underwater. When alarmed, it slaps water with its tail as a warning to other beavers. Gnaws trees until they fall: for food; for building materials for bowshaped dams; for domelike lodges; and for scent mounds, which mark territory and attract mates. Burrows up through snow to gnaw trees at surface; as snow level changes, several gnawed bands may be left, creating a "totem pole" effect. Active throughout year. Feeds mostly on aspen, cottonwood, willow, and birch. Will also eat cattails, tules, willow roots, pond lilies. Its droppings of coarse, sawdustlike material are rarely found because they decompose rapidly. Probably mates for life. Kits born furred, eyes open, four per litter. Stay with parents for two years. Lifespan 10-12 years. Young killed by otters. Adults occasionally killed by coyotes, foxes, bobcats, and lions. Almost trapped out of existence in nineteenth century to supply soft, fine fur for hats, robes, and coats, now reestablished over most of its former range.

113-130mm

$\frac{1\ 0\ 1\ 3}{1\ 0\ 1\ 3}$

hind 165mm

top view of molar

Droppings: 35-40mm, rarely found.

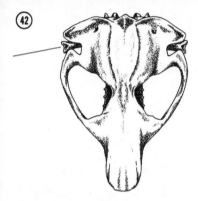

56-62mm

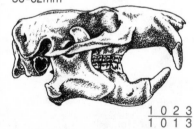

$$\frac{1\ 0\ 2\ 3}{1\ 0\ 1\ 3}$$

Mountain Beaver
Aplodontia rufa

Dark brown above, lighter below, nearly tailless. Not really a beaver. Its burrow entrances, to 20 cm across, sometimes have a tent of twigs covered with leaves and fern fronds erected over them. Nips branches near burrow entrances. Its tunnels are shallow, prone to collapsing, often leading to food and water. Eats mostly bark, ferns (especially bracken and swordfern) and creates "haypiles" to dry plants for nests and food. Reingests droppings. Active at night, autumn days. Climbs trees. Voice a shrill whistle, rarely heard. Females breed at two years; one litter of three to five is born in spring. Enemies: bobcats, long-tailed weasels, mink.

15mm

hind 55–63mm

no visible tail

(43)

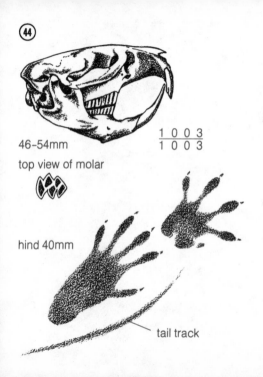

(44)

46–54mm

top view of molar

$$\frac{1\ 0\ 0\ 3}{1\ 0\ 0\ 3}$$

hind 40mm

tail track

Muskrat
Ondatra zibethica

Aquatic rodent with dark brown, glossy fur. Naked tail is flattened vertically for swimming. Excellent swimmer, stays submerged for 15 minutes. Mouth closes behind protruding incisors, making underwater chewing possible. Builds house of matted vegetation to 1.2 m high; burrows in banks; makes feeding platforms. Marks territory with mats of cut plants where scent is spread. Active day and night. Eats aquatic plants, clams, crayfish, frogs, fish. Breeds April-August, has up to five litters per year of four to seven naked, blind young. Babies swim at one week. Live five-six years. Raccoons, otters, mink, and people are major enemies.

Droppings: 10–13mm, rarely found.

Porcupine
Erethizon dorsatum

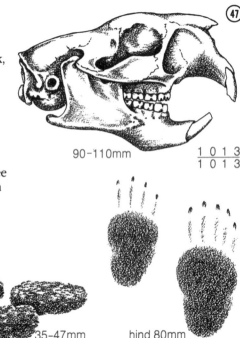

Gray-brown, chunky body, high arching back, short legs. Has about 30,000 hair quills on back, rump and tail. When alarmed, flips tail, releasing quills from skin. Quills are not thrown. Once in an enemy's flesh, the quills work deeper, can be fatal. Porcupine has no other defense. In forests and some open areas. Active year-around. Mostly nocturnal, but suns in trees. Solitary in summer, lives colonially in winter. Eats green plants and inside layer of tree bark. Fond of salt. Mates in fall. One baby born May or June, headfirst, with soft quills aimed backward. Fishers are good at flipping porcupines over to expose their vulnerable bellies; mountain lions, coyotes, bobcats also attack them.

90-110mm

$$\frac{1 \quad 0 \quad 1 \quad 3}{1 \quad 0 \quad 1 \quad 3}$$

quill magnified

35-47mm

hind 80mm

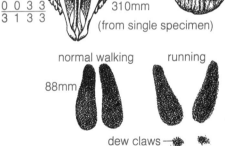

bone core without horn sheath · with horn sheath

Bighorn Sheep
Ovis canadensis

Gray-brown to ash gray; belly, rump white. Horns in rams thick, coiled; in ewes, not coiled, small. Sexes separate in summer, together in fall. Rams of equal size challenge each other for ewes, rear and charge at 20 mph to butt heads loudly. Skull double thick with struts of bone to cushion impact. Eats sedge, grass, sagebrush, alpine plants. Bed a depression smelling of urine with droppings along edges, used for years. Single lamb born May-June, stays with herd. Lives 14 years. Golden eagles take lambs. Threatened by weather, disease, loss of viable habitat, intrusion. Several isolated races or populations occur.

$\frac{0\ 0\ 3\ 3}{3\ 1\ 3\ 3}$ 310mm
(from single specimen)

13-16mm
Cakes: 80mm.

normal walking   running

88mm

dew claws →

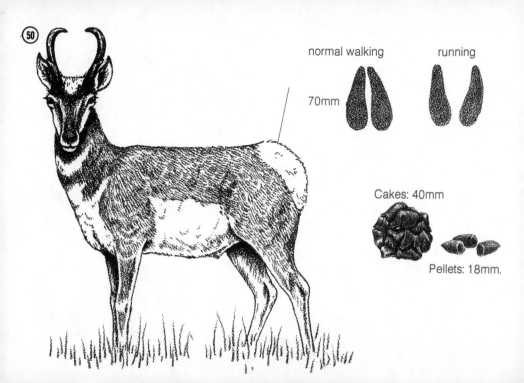

normal walking

running

70mm

Cakes: 40mm

Pellets: 18mm.

Pronghorn Antelope
Antilocapra americana

Upper body tan; chest, belly, rump white. Short, erect mane. Antelope raises rump hairs to flash warning when alarmed. Sheds outer covering of horns after breeding season, permanent core remains. Can run at 44 mph, with short bursts to 70 mph — fastest animal in western hemisphere. Can leap horizontally four to eight meters, but can't jump fences. In open prairies, sagebrush plains. Forms summer bands up to 12 animals; winter bands to 100. Eats grasses, cacti, sagebrush, rabbitbrush. Droppings are in segmented masses when antelope eats succulent grass, small pebble-like forms when it browses. Antelope, breeds in fall. Young born April-June, unspotted, odorless. Twins common. Lifespan 10 years. Chief enemy: coyotes.

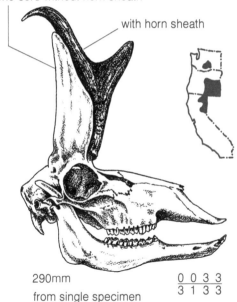

bone core without horn sheath

with horn sheath

290mm
from single specimen

$$\frac{0\ 0\ 3\ 3}{3\ 1\ 3\ 3}$$

Mule Deer
Odocoileus hemionus

Coat varies: yellow-brown, sooty-gray, blue-gray. Tail white with black tip, to all black. Rump patch white. 100-400 pounds. Antlers: branched; number of branches and rack size increase with age, decline after peak; are shed in winter; grown again in early spring, are covered with velvet until late summer. Buck damages saplings and branches by rubbing off velvet. Mule deer are active most hours except mid-day. Chiefly a browser; fond of clover, alfalfa, acorns, many shrubs.

Coastal deer lose weight June-November, followed by natural die-off. Survivors gain weight after fall rains. Shrubs resprouting after fires in the fall, combined with available acorns, supply deer with essential food for recovery.

Bucks solitary; may form bands before and after mating season. Harems form in

Pellets: 12-18mm.

Cakes: 67mm.

October. Spotless, odorless fawns are born May-June, hidden for one month. Young does have singles, older does twins. Fawns, yearlings travel in family groups with mothers. Bucks urinate in beds as they stand; does step to one side first. Chief enemies: lions, bobcats, coyotes, domestic dogs, people, and cars. Six subspecies.

winter

spring

summer
(in velvet)

Six subspecies recognized by tail differences:

California   Southern   Inyo   Rocky Mt.   Burro   Columbian Black-tailed

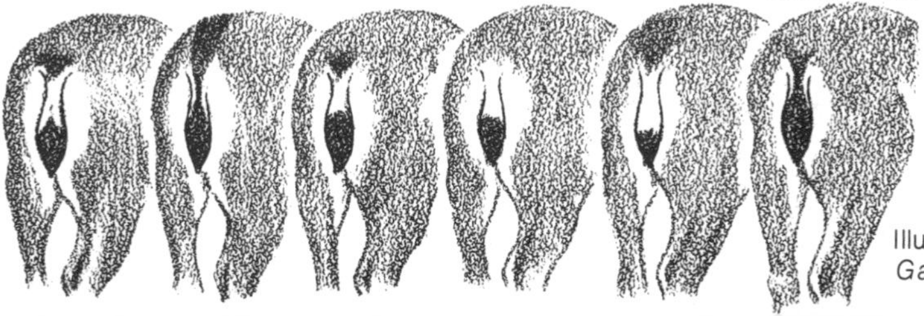

More illustrations on next page.

Illustration based on one in *Big Game of California,* see p 92.

mule and
white-tailed

running

dew claws

walking

63-82mm

54

Mule Deer

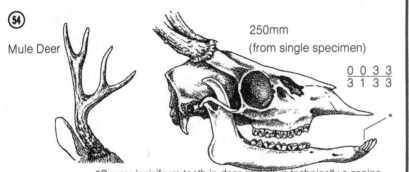

250mm
(from single specimen)

$$\frac{0\ \ 0\ \ 3\ \ 3}{3\ \ 1\ \ 3\ \ 3}$$

*

*Corner incisiform tooth in deer and elk is technically a canine.

White-tailed Deer

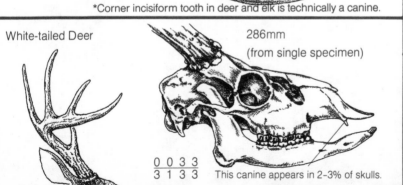

286mm
(from single specimen)

$$\frac{0\ \ 0\ \ 3\ \ 3}{3\ \ 1\ \ 3\ \ 3}$$

This canine appears in 2-3% of skulls.

White-tailed Deer
Flag-tail
Odocoileus virginianus

Coat reddish in summer, blue-gray in
winter. Raises all-white tail when running.
In forests, brushlands, swampy
meadowlands. Home range about one mile.
Runs to 40 mph. Jumps nine meters
horizontally, 2.4 m high. Bucks rub antlers
on tree trunks and saplings close to ground
to mark territory, remove velvet, and to
sharpen them. Breed November-February.
Adult does often have twins. White-tailed
deer stamps feet and snorts when nervous.
Lives 16 years in wild. Rips vegetation away,
rather than nipping as rabbits do. Same
enemies as other deer. Two sub-species in
our area.

Pellets: 12–28mm.   Cakes: 48mm.

(56)

C. canadensis   *C. nannodes*

chew marks

Wapiti, Canadian Elk
Cervus canadensis
Tule Elk
C. nannodes

$$\frac{0\ \ 1\ \ 3\ \ 3}{3\ \ 1\ \ 3\ \ 3}$$

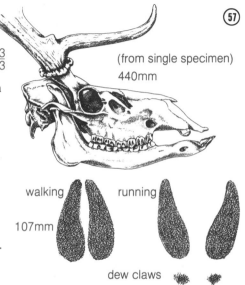

(from single specimen)
440mm

Tail and rump patch is tawny in wapiti; white in tule (Canadian) elk. Males to 1,000 pounds, females smaller. Habitat: mountain meadows in summer, lower wooded areas in winter. Tule elk prefer marshes, river bottoms, open plains. Active dusk to dawn. Can run 35 mph. Primarily grazers. In mixed groups of 25 or so in winter. Older bucks separate in summer. During breeding season (rut) August-November, bucks bugle loudly to challenge rivals and gather harems of up to 60 females. Bulls weakened after breeding go into hiding to avoid predators. Shed antlers February-March; new antlers start in April. Mountain lion is chief enemy. Bears, coyotes take calves. Wapiti were once slaughtered for their two upper canine "bugler" teeth, which were used for watch charms.

walking   running

107mm

dew claws

Pellets: 18–35mm.   Cakes: 110mm

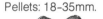

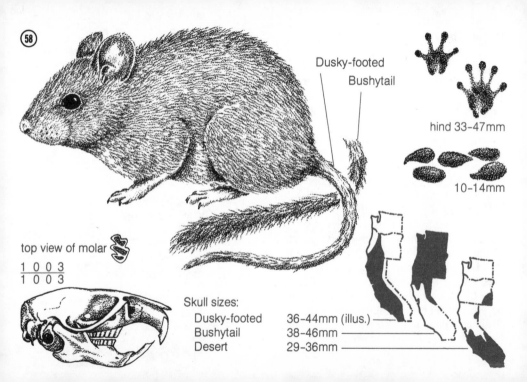

(58)

Dusky-footed

Bushytail

hind 33–47mm

10–14mm

top view of molar

$$\frac{1\ 0\ 0\ 3}{1\ 0\ 0\ 3}$$

Skull sizes:
Dusky-footed   36–44mm (illus.)
Bushytail   38–46mm
Desert   29–36mm

Woodrats

Presence of gray-tawny woodrats is indicated by bulky nests of twigs at bases of trees, shrubs, in rock crevices, in cactus or tree branches. Earn name "packrat" by stashing anything they fancy in their nests. Nocturnal, territorial, they respond to disturbance by drumming or thumping with hind feet or tails. Woodrat tails have hairs, unlike "old world" rats. Feed on green plants, nuts, seeds, fruit, fungi. Most species give birth to one to four young per annual litter. Enemies include owls, foxes, coyotes, bobcats and large snakes.

Desert Woodrat, *(Neotoma lepida),* may have four litters per year. It defends prickly pear patches for food and water during the dry season.

Dusky-footed Woodrat, *(N. fuscipes),* often builds a second "escape" nest in tree branches near ground nest.

Bushytail Woodrat, *(N. cinerea),* accumulates various materials in rock crevices or under logs in high mountain areas.

(Real nests would not be so near each other.)

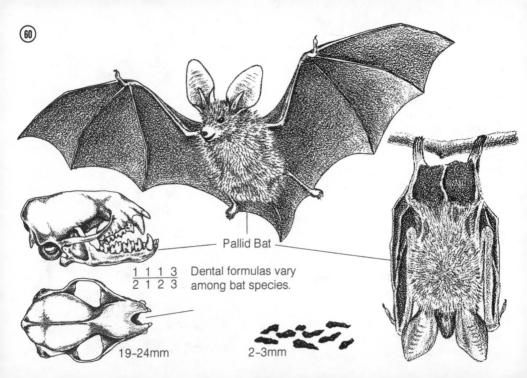

Pallid Bat

$\frac{1\ 1\ 1\ 3}{2\ 1\ 2\ 3}$ Dental formulas vary among bat species.

19-24mm

2-3mm

Bats

Twenty-five species in our area. Only true flying mammals. Furry bodies, naked wings. Hearing is acute. To avoid objects and locate food, bats depend on emission of sounds from nose or mouth, at rate of 30-60 squeaks per second, that echo back off objects. Muscles control ears so that bats hear only returning sound waves when flying. Bats capture insects in flight or on ground, consuming tons of destructive pests. Drink from streams, ponds, lakes in flight; often captured by large trout, bass. Feed around city street lights; hang on porch walls and eat large insects, leaving droppings on walls. Hang head down. Metabolism lowered when asleep to conserve energy. Some bats are solitary, others colonial. Some migrate, others hibernate. One or two young born late spring. Some bats carry rabies, so handling them is dangerous.

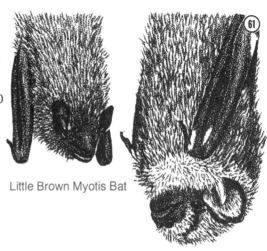

Little Brown Myotis Bat

Hoary Bat

Opossum
Didelphis marsupialis

Only pouched mammal in U.S. Scruffy, gray body with prehensile tail. Thin, black, hairless ears and part of tail may be missing in north range, due to freezing. Opossum feigns death when threatened. Thrives in urban, rural, and woodland areas. Nests in hollow trees, logs, culverts, brush piles, under houses. Eats fruit, vegetables, nuts, insects, carrion, eggs. Nocturnal. Solitary. Does not hibernate; stays in den for several weeks in cold weather. Has one to two litters, January to October. One to 14 embryos crawl out of womb to pouch covering 13 teats. All could fit in teaspoon. Nurse for two months. Five to seven normally survive to juvenile stage. Lifespan about seven years.

hind 60-79mm

116-127mm

$$\frac{5 \ 1 \ 3 \ 4}{4 \ 1 \ 3 \ 4}$$

small brain case

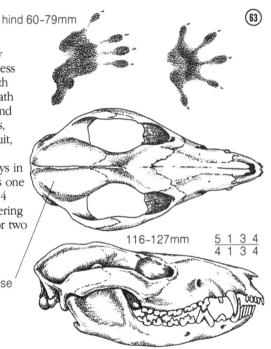

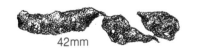

42mm

Spotted Skunk
Spilogale putorius

Boldly marked, with pom-pom-like tail. More active than other skunks. Stands on front feet with back and tail arched over head as defense warning. Climbs trees to escape enemies. One spotted skunk may range over 160 acres. Less territorial than other skunks, more socially tolerant, thus 13 or more spotted skunks may be found in a square mile. Nests in burrows beneath buildings, rock piles. Several may den together in winter. Feeds on mice, birds, eggs, insects, carrion, and some vegetable matter. Mates in September. Two to seven young born May-June. Great horned owls, cars are worst enemies; foxes and bobcats take a few.

hind 39-55mm

$$\frac{3 \quad 1 \quad 3 \quad 1}{3 \quad 1 \quad 3 \quad 2}$$

30-40mm

51-62mm

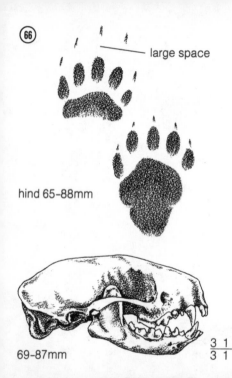

large space

hind 65-88mm

69-87mm

$\frac{3\ 1\ 3\ 1}{3\ 1\ 3\ 2}$

Striped Skunk
Mephitis mephitis

Bold coloring warns predators. When threatened may snarl, stamp feet, raise hindlegs, click teeth, arch tail, turn toward enemy. This failing, shoots a jet spray of musk (to 4.5 meters) as final defense. Adult skunk needs about 10 acres. Uses abandoned burrows of other animals, digs its own or may use protected spaces under houses (unless repelled by mothballs). Nocturnal. Does not hibernate; may be inactive for weeks in winter. Males solitary; females may den together in winter. Eats variety of vegetable matter, insects, grubs, mice, eggs, frogs, and also yellowjackets and their nests, leaving large holes in ground. Four to seven young born in May, follow mother single-file until June or July. Chief carrier of rabies. Predators: great horned owls, golden eagles.

30-44mm

68

River Otter
Lutra canadensis

Color rich brown above, silvery below. Can stay underwater two to three minutes because pulse slows and skin flaps close ears and nostrils. Lives in large rivers, streams, sloughs, or along seashore in northern areas. Home range 15 miles. Travels at night. Enlarges and uses burrows of other animals, such as beaver, muskrat, for dens along water's edge. Makes river bank slides 30 cm wide. Snow slides show track marks. When on land, spends most of its time frollicking, chasing tail, or playing tag. Rolls in tules or grass to dry off and to mark territory with musk, droppings. Females breed again just after giving birth, in March to May, to one to four blind, helpless, furry pups which must be taught to swim. Eats fish.

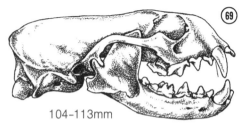

(69)

104-113mm

$$\frac{3 \quad 1 \quad 4 \quad 1}{3 \quad 1 \quad 3 \quad 2}$$

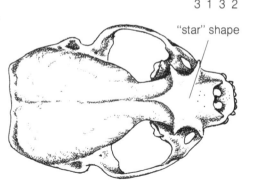

"star" shape

hind 100-146mm

Droppings: 60-65mm, rarely found.

Pine Marten

Martes americana

Brown body with orange-yellow throat and chest. Lives in deep coniferous forests, large high-mountain rock piles. Dens in hollow trees. Active night, early morning, late afternoon and cloudy days. Spends lots of time in trees. May range 15 miles in search of food. Eats tree squirrels, mice, voles, pikas, hares, some berries. Buries surplus meat. Breeds in mid-summer; fertilization of eggs by sperm is delayed, embryos form in early winter. Young born in April, one to five in litter. May breed after first year. Males use scent glands under belly skin to mark territory, attract mate. Martens are curious. One male was live-trapped 77 times in a row. Enemies include fisher, large owls.

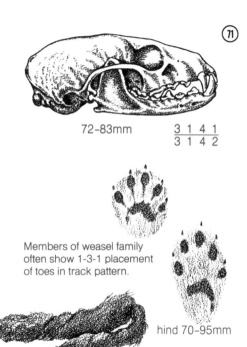

72-83mm

$$\frac{3\ 1\ 4\ 1}{3\ 1\ 4\ 2}$$

Members of weasel family often show 1-3-1 placement of toes in track pattern.

hind 70–95mm

55mm

Long-tailed Weasel
Mustela frenata

Body brown, with black face and tail tip, underparts beige-yellow, except in snow country, northern areas, where shorter fall days stimulate color change to all white with black nose, eyes, and tail tip. Habitat varied: forest, brush, farmland, near water. Chiefly nocturnal, but active in day and night, throughout year. Eats mostly mice — often caches several dead mice under log. Also eats rabbits, squirrels, chipmunks, birds, etc. Most ferocious, efficient mammal predator, ounce for ounce. Leaves droppings on logs, rocks, stumps. Lines nest, in abandoned den of other animal, with fur of mice and "trophies" (bones, feathers) of hunts. Three to nine nearly naked, blind young are born in May. Enemies: hawks, owls, cats, coyotes, foxes, mink, marten, fisher.

50mm (from one specimen)

$$\frac{3\ 1\ 3\ 1}{3\ 1\ 3\ 2}$$

hind 35-47mm

28mm

Badger
Taxidea taxus

Coat yellow-grizzled gray. Eyesight poor. Strong senses of smell and hearing. Loose skin allows twisting, turning in tight spaces to catch food, defend self. In arid grassland in nearly all life zones. It digs to catch food, escape, rest, den, and to bury droppings and extra food. Its burrow entrance is 20 to 30 cm wide, elliptical, with flat bottom. Eats rabbits, gophers, squirrels, mice, rattlesnakes, yellowjackets. Coyotes may follow badgers to steal the prey they flush from burrows. Badger is solitary, active day or night. May sleep for weeks during cold weather. Changes dens almost daily in summer. One to five cubs born blind, furred, in February to May. Enemies are bears and lions, who do not find badgers easy prey. Their squat forms, sharp teeth, strong neck muscles are major defensive tools.

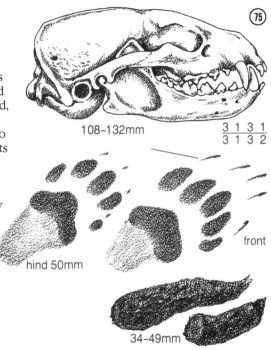

(75)

108-132mm

$$\frac{3\ 1\ 3\ 1}{3\ 1\ 3\ 2}$$

hind 50mm

front

34-49mm

Raccoon
Procyon lotor

Color salt-and-pepper. Playful, curious, good swimmer. Feeds mostly along streams, lakes, ponds, but will wander from water. Dens in hollow trees, logs, rock crevices, or ground burrows. In cold weather, may sleep for several days; does not hibernate. Chiefly nocturnal, but occasionally about in day. Especially active in autumn. Solitary except when breeding, caring for young. Diet varied: fruits, nuts, grains, insects, frogs, fish, crayfish, birds' eggs. Washing food enhances sense of touch in toes, helps raccoon discern non-edible matter. Leaves droppings at base of den tree, on large branches, rocks, logs across streams. Mates in February or March. Two to seven young born April or May. In fall, young raccoons may disperse up to 160 miles, but mostly less than 30 miles. Chief enemies: dogs, hunters, autos. Raccoon can defend self well against a single dog.

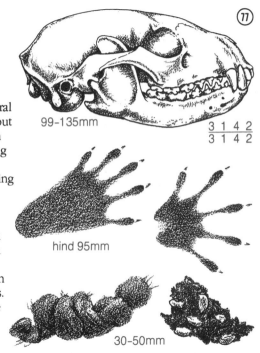

99–135mm

$\frac{3\ 1\ 4\ 2}{3\ 1\ 4\ 2}$

hind 95mm

30–50mm

claw marks

Black Bear
Ursus americanus

Body black or cinnamon. Has keen sense of smell, climbs trees easily. Can run 30 mph in short bursts. Can range 15 miles. Dens under downed trees, hollow logs or trees, other shelter. Solitary, except when breeding and in garbage dumps. Mainly vegetarian, but also eats fish, small mammals, eggs, carrion, honeycomb, bees, garbage. Does not hibernate. In fall, bears add thick layer of fat to sustain them during winter sleep; bears without enough fat are active during winter. Mates June to July, every other year. Two to three cubs born in winter den. Lifespan 30 years. "Bear trees" have tooth marks as high as bear stands; claw marks above, to mark territory. Bears are dangerous when: surprised, hungry, feeding, injured, or with cubs. Use of claws, pancreas as mythical aphrodisiacs is causing deline of bears outside parks.

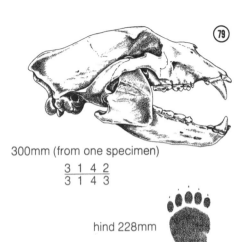

300mm (from one specimen)

$$\frac{3\ 1\ 4\ 2}{3\ 1\ 4\ 3}$$

hind 228mm

80-110mm

hind 57mm

Coyote
Canis latrans

Color and size variable. Mountain coyotes are larger, have longer fur than desert coyotes. Coyote is vocal at night — a series of yaps, a long howl, then short yaps. Holds tail between legs when running. Can reach 40 mph. Track like a dog's. Population, range increasing despite hunting, poisoning campaigns. Widespread. Dens along river banks, well-drained sides of canyons, gulches. May enlarge badger or squirrel burrows. Chiefly nocturnal, but active any time. Often hunts in pairs. Omnivorous, but mostly eats small rodents, rabbits, squirrels. Droppings gray, with some seeds, but mostly fur, bones, insect parts, reptile skin, feathers; occasionally solid foil, plastic, or grass, which helps remove tapeworms. Mates January-February. Six to seven pups born April to May, raised by both parents. Livestock losses blamed on coyotes often the work of dogs. Coyotes kill many grass-eating rodents, earning protection from some ranchers.

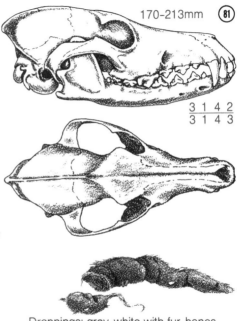

170-213mm (81)

$$\frac{3\ 1\ 4\ 2}{3\ 1\ 4\ 3}$$

Droppings: gray-white with fur, bones, insect parts, 55–88mm long, 20mm diam.

hind 44mm

San Joaquin Kit Fox
Vulpes macrotis

Color sandy, tawny-gray. Mainly nocturnal, but active during day in deserts. Hot weather forces it into burrow, 23 cm across, which it digs for itself in sandy soil, or it uses abandoned badger's den. Eats rodents, rabbits, insects, lizards, snakes. Uses stalk-and-pounce strategy. Very quick, reaches 25 mph. Four to five pups born February-March. Both parents raise young; while female cares for them, male hunts, returns with food. Family disperses in autumn. Eagles and coyotes are main enemies. In San Joaquin Valley, this fox is chief predator of rodents on agricultural land. Poison baits intended for coyotes kill many foxes, and their loss results in survival of high numbers of rodents that damage crops.

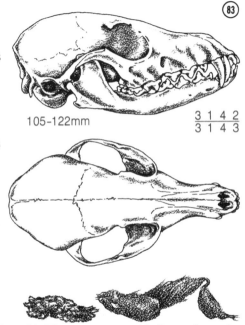

105-122mm

$\frac{3\ 1\ 4\ 2}{3\ 1\ 4\ 3}$

Droppings: 31–69mm, may resemble those of gray fox.

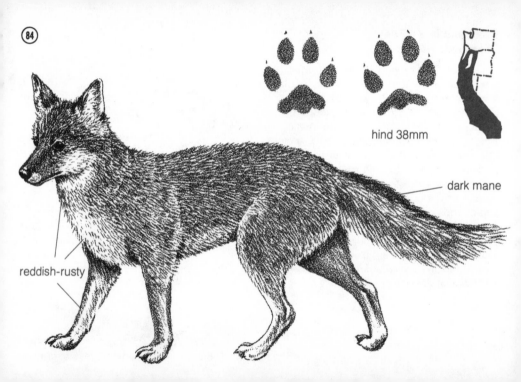

(84)

hind 38mm

dark mane

reddish-rusty

Gray Fox
Urocyon cinereoargenteus

Salt-and-pepper gray with rusty neck, legs, feet. Less vocal than other foxes. Can run, in short bursts, 28 mph. Only fox which climbs trees to escape or to hunt. Mainly in woodland, chaparral. Dens in hollow trees, logs, under rock ledges, or in culverts; may have several escape dens nearby. Den area often marked by accumulation of droppings, bones. Gray fox is nocturnal, but often seen in day. Eats small rodents, insects, birds, eggs, fruit, acorns; in some areas, diet is largely cottontail rabbits, ground squirrels, berries. Two to seven pups are born March-April, dark brown, eyes closed. Hunt on their own at four months. Afflicted with many diseases, parasitic worms. Enemies: domestic dogs, bobcats, lions, people. Poison bait intended for coyotes kills many gray foxes.

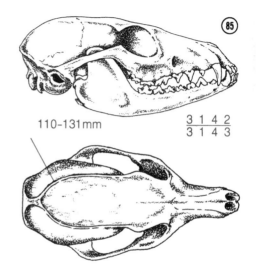

85

110-131mm

$$\frac{3\ 1\ 4\ 2}{3\ 1\ 4\ 3}$$

Droppings: 50mm, 10mm diam., smaller than coyote's, almost always black with stringy ends, berry seeds, fur, etc.

(86)

hind 50 mm

white

nearly black legs/feet

Red Fox
Vulpes vulpes

Rusty-red, but several color phases exist. White-tipped tail a key feature. In cultivated land, wooded areas, brushland, high mountains. Range is expanding. Mostly nocturnal, also active early morning, evening. Eats fruit, insects, crayfish in summer; birds, mice, rabbits, squirrels in winter. Adults remain solitary until breeding time. Den usually in open area, or along stream, in rock pile. May use enlarged den of badger or marmot. Entrance one foot wide, with fan of packed dirt, bones, droppings; one to three smaller, less conspicuous escape holes nearby. Establishes den after mating in January-February, abandons it by late August when family disperses. Four to eight pups born March-May. After several weeks, parents deliver live prey so pups can practice killing. Young males disperse up to 150 miles from birthplace. Enemies: bobcats, coyotes, golden eagles, people.

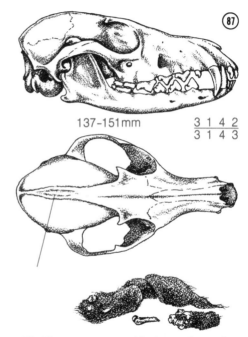

137–151mm

$$\frac{3\ 1\ 4\ 2}{3\ 1\ 4\ 3}$$

Droppings: 50–63mm, may resemble those of gray fox.

Bobcat
Felis rufus

Gray-brown to reddish. Ear tufts used like antennae to aid hearing. Good climber. Gets name from "bobbed" tail. In almost every habitat, life zone. Range is usually within two miles, may be up to 50 miles. Mostly nocturnal, also seen in daytime. Solitary. Often rests on branches, atop large rocks to watch for passing prey. Eats rabbits, mice, squirrels, porcupines, woodrats, cave bats, small, weak deer. Caches large kills. Droppings are like dog's or coyote's, but often partially buried, with scratch marks on ground. One to seven (average two to three) kittens born April-May in den of dry leaves in hollow log, under rock ledge or fallen tree. Southern animals may have two litters per year. Lifespan 25 years. Marks territory by urinating on rocks or tree trunks, making scent posts. Uses tree trunk as scratching post. Often killed by poison bait intended for coyotes.

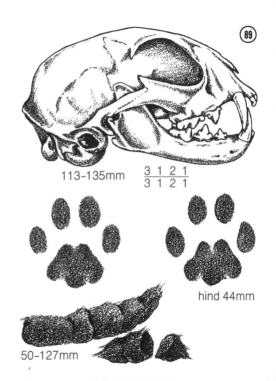

113-135mm $\frac{3\ 1\ 2\ 1}{3\ 1\ 2\ 1}$

hind 44mm

50-127mm

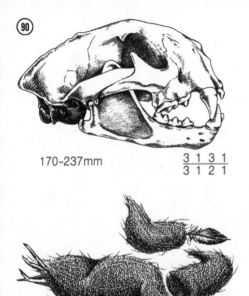

170–237mm

$$\frac{3}{3} \frac{1}{1} \frac{3}{2} \frac{1}{1}$$

Droppings: 76–228mm. Form pellet droppings in desert. All cat droppings are partially buried.

Mountain Lion, Cougar, Puma

Felis concolor

Yellowish, grayish, reddish-tawny. Habitat generally wilderness but may hunt in rural hills. Male may travel 25 miles in one night. Strongly territorial. Mostly nocturnal. Rarely seen. Voice like tomcat's, greatly magnified. Uses tree trunks as scratching posts. Solitary, except in two week breeding season. Eats large mammals; one deer per week forms half of diet. Has more success catching old, weak, less alert deer, thus keeps herd healthy. Also eats coyotes, porcupines, beavers, rabbits, marmots, raccoons, birds, sometimes livestock. Covers remains of large kill with branches, leaves. Droppings often left like bobcat's. Adults breed every two-three years. One to six furry, spotted kittens born midsummer, raised by female for one to two years. Only enemy is man. Before lions were legally protected, I met a man with 52 lion skulls, from animals killed in the Kern River Canyon — a tragic waste. Protection should be permanent, even though population is reported to be increasing.

hind 101mm

91

Allen, Thomas. *Wild Animals of North America*. National Geographic Society, 1979

Berry, William and Elizabeth. *Mammals of the San Francisco Bay Region*. University of California Press, 1959

Burt, William H. and Richard P. Grossenheider. *A Field Guide to the Mammals*. Houghton Mifflin, 1976

Dasmann, William. *Big Game of California*. California Department of Fish and Game, 1958

Grater, Russell. *Discovering Sierra Mammals*. Yosemite Natural History Association, 1978

Haley, Delphine. *Sleek and Savage: North America's Weasel Family*. Pacific Search Press, 1975

Ingles, Lloyd. *Mammals of the Pacific States*. Stanford University press, 1965

Kritzman, Ellen. *Little Mammals of the Pacific Northwest*. Pacific Search Press, 1977

Mays, Buddy. *Guide to Western Wildlife: A Pilgrim's Notebook*. Chronicle Books, 1977

Murie, Olaus. *A Field Guide to Animal Tracks*. Houghton Mifflin, 1974

Rue, Leonard Lee. *Pictorial Guide to the Mammals of North America*. Crowell, 1967

Schmidt, John L. and Douglas L. Gilbert, eds. *Big Game of North America*. Stackpole Books, 1980

Seymour, George. *Furbearers of California*. California Department Department of Fish and Game, 1977

Vaughan, Terry. *Mammalogy*. W.B. Saunders Co., 1972

Wallmo, Olof C., ed. *Mule and Blacktailed Deer of North America*. University of Nebraska Press, 1981

Whitaker, John. *The Audubon Society Field Guide to North American Mammals*. Knopf, 1980

other books like this one, and what they identify

for North America east of the Rocky Mountains:

FLOWER FINDER — spring wildflowers and flower families
TREE FINDER — all native and introduced trees
WINTER TREE FINDER — leafless winter trees
FERN FINDER — native northeastern and midwestern ferns
TRACK FINDER — tracks and footprints of mammals
BERRY FINDER — native plants with fleshy fruits
LIFE ON INTERTIDAL ROCKS — intertidal organisms
WINTER WEED FINDER — dry plants in winter

for the Pacific coast states:

PACIFIC COAST TREE FINDER — native trees, Sitka to San Diego
PACIFIC COAST BIRD FINDER — 61 common birds
PACIFIC COAST BERRY FINDER — native plants with fleshy fruits
PACIFIC COAST FERN FINDER — native ferns and fern relatives
REDWOOD REGION FLOWER FINDER — wildflowers and families
SIERRA FLOWER FINDER — wildflowers of the Sierra Nevada
PACIFIC INTERTIDAL LIFE — organisms of pools, rocks and reefs
MAMMAL FINDER — mammals and their signs

also:

DESERT TREE FINDER — trees of southwestern deserts
ROCKY MOUNTAIN TREE FINDER — native trees of Rocky Mountains

for a catalog write NATURE STUDY GUILD, Box 972, Berkeley, California 94701